The Monarch's Progress

Poems with Wings

Written and Illustrated by

Avis Harley

WORDSONG

Honesdale, Pennsylvania

In loving memory of my mother,
who first opened my eyes
to the world of butterflies
—A.H.

The publisher thanks Lincoln Brower, Ph.D., research professor of biology, Sweet Briar College and Distinguished Service Professor of Zoology, Emeritus, University of Florida, for reviewing the text and illustrations of this book for accuracy.

Wordsong
An Imprint of Boyds Mills Press, Inc.
815 Church Street
Honesdale, Pennsylvania 18431
Printed in China

CIP data is available.

ISBN-13: 978-1-59078-558-4

First edition
The text of this book is set in 15-point Sabon.
The illustrations are done in pencil.

10 9 8 7 6 5 4 3 2 1

CONTENTS

INTRODUCTION

Why are butterflies so universally loved?

Is it because of the dazzling art and colors in their wings? Or their amazing feats of flight? Or is the miracle of change what fascinates us—that wonderful metamorphosis from tiny egg to brilliant insect?

I discovered while working on *The Monarch's Progress* that poetry writing is much like the four stages in this metamorphosis: the poet starts with a tiny spark of an idea (*egg*); chews through a multitude of thoughts (*caterpillar*); allows the idea to grow, change, and develop (*chrysalis*); then releases the poem in its final form (*imago*).

Wanting to emphasize those four words, I spelled them out in the first letter of each line in the acrostic poems "Monarch Beginnings," "Worldly Wise," "Getting Ready," and "Final Finery." Part of the fun of poetry writing is exploring different poetic forms and seeing how the subject of a poem will determine its shape.

The poem "Chaos" called for a cumulative format, showing the butterfly effect increasing in size until it reached hurricane proportions. A zigzag shape for "Catching a Butterfly (1)" illustrated the darting motions of a monarch in flight. In "Wintering Over," *A* to *Z* formed the first letters of every line, creating an abecedarian poem. This long, vertical poem echoed the outline of a long branch weighted down with butterflies.

I included a summary of some amazing facts about the monarch in the final section, Small Matters. Readers will discover that this butterfly lays several hundred eggs, that the caterpillar increases its weight by three thousand times, and that migrating monarchs will fly 2,500 miles (4,000 kilometers) to reach their winter roosts.

There are thousands of different kinds of butterflies. Do you have a favorite—one that you have observed in real life or maybe seen in a book? You might like to write a poem about this butterfly and capture it in a word picture. Try describing it in a way that nobody has thought of before: you'll create poetry on the wing!

SIPPING SUPPER

Open
the friendly smile
of a watermelon
and celebrate the sunny taste
inside.

Why not
ask the monarchs
to hover on over
and share a sip or two of sweet
summer?

FEET TREAT

How handy are the monarch's taste-full feet
reporting where the nectar treasure flows!
Whenever they have savored something sweet,
they phone Proboscis to uncoil the hose.

This gives the butterfly a lovely straw
to carry out her dainty floral sips.
So delicately does she drink and draw,
she never needs to nectar up her lips.

Imagine if we tasted with our toes—
what grounded flavors do you think we'd find?
A crush of mint leaves? Sunbaked seaweed? Snows?
Sweet dew? Or apples summer left behind?

If we would let our toes seek what we eat,
what smorgasbord would greet our eager feet?

CATCHING A BUTTERFLY (1)

Draw.
    Color.
        Bright!
            Dark!
                Remembering
                    a monarch
                        dart
                        in the
                    park.
                With
            just
        a line
    around
    this
        thought,
            she
                colors
                    between ...
                            and
                        the
                        scene
                    is
                caught.

CATCHING A BUTTERFLY (2)

Stone-grown for a Pharaoh's room,
the butterfly rises in its tomb.

Forever must this lovely thing
soar within a sunless spring.

Caught upon a buried sky,
millennia have passed it by.

Yet still, across the muted years,
a whisper of wing haunts our ears.

MONARCH BEGINNINGS

No bigger than the head of a pin, though
Enough to house a lodger within. Oh!
What a drama about to begin!

Exquisite gem on a milkweed leaf—your
Gorgeous shell-life is all too brief, for
Growing inside is a caterpillar thief . . .

WORLDLY WISE

Comma-size
And worldly wise,
The tiny caterpillar arrives
Eager to feed on leafy green—
Ravenous, greedy feasting machine!
Plumping up until it splits to shed
Its skin for one that fits—
Lively stripes grow bold in rows as
Larger and larger the larva grows.
And then—it ends this gorging bliss,
Retiring as a chrysalis.

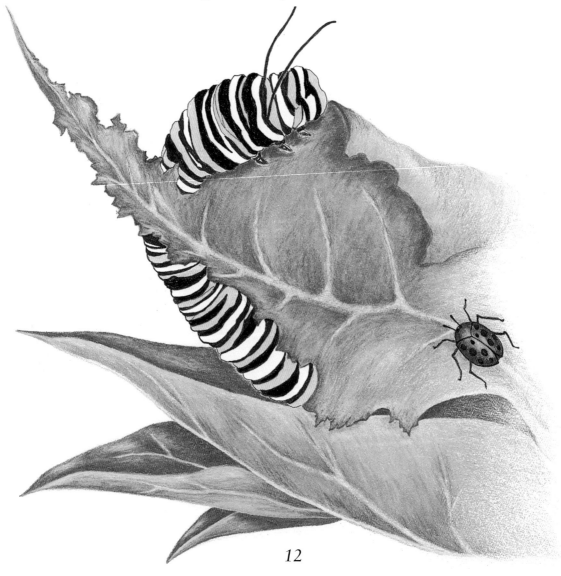

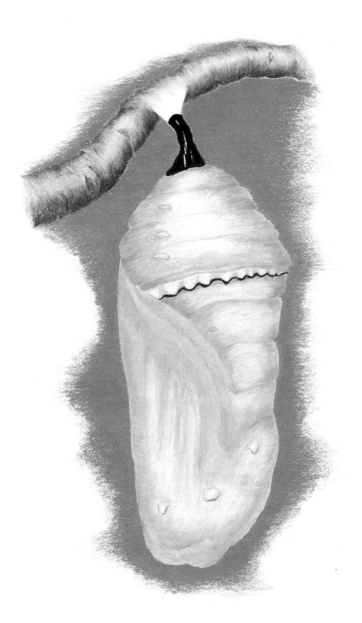

GETTING READY

Caterpillar spins a silken button to
Hold its home in place. Then upside down,
Removes its cloak and dons a chrysalis case.
Yesterday's grub, now dressed in green,
Serenely hides the inside scene, where
Adult wings and
Long legs grow—designing an
Insect fashion
Show.

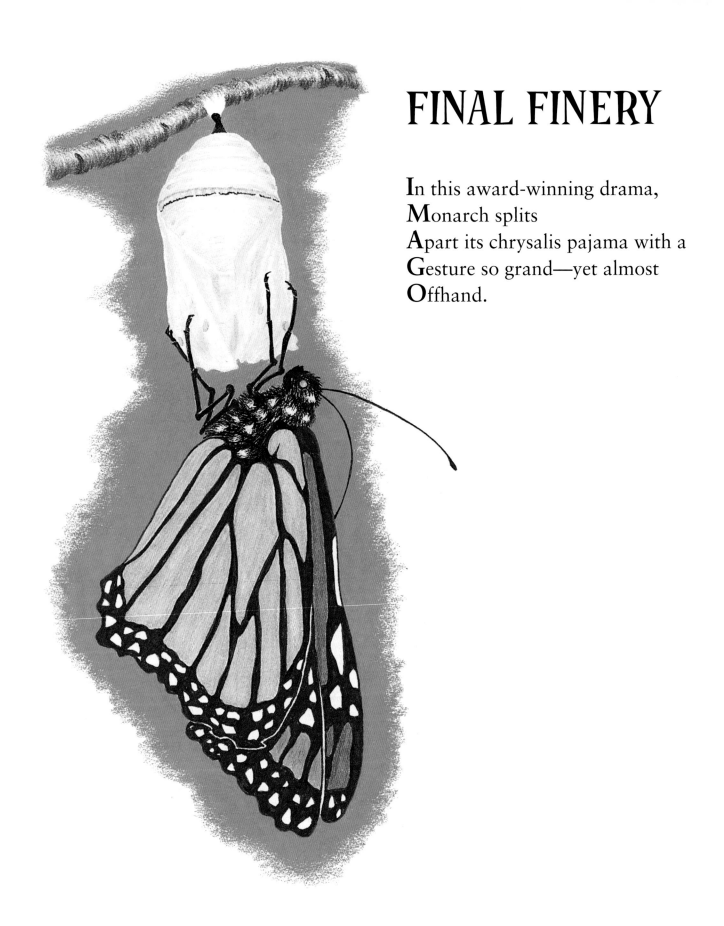

FINAL FINERY

In this award-winning drama,
Monarch splits
Apart its chrysalis pajama with a
Gesture so grand—yet almost
Offhand.

Who can decorate
the walls of the world better
than a butterfly?

OPPOSITES

For the butterfly, all is delight!
Life is courtship and nectar and flight—
and that glittering dress:
how it seems to possess
orange pieces of sun laced with night!

But the larva is truly a bore
for its life is made up of one chore:
all it does is chew leaves
while the mother plant grieves
at this loss to her greenery store.

What a marvelous contrast they are:
one is shaped like a heavy cigar
while the other is dainty.
Though they both are quite painty,
one is ground-bound, the other a star.

YOU'VE GOT MALE

Lion prowls through his jungle domain
looking proud as a peacock, and vain.
He's so macho-superb
he has earned his own verb.
How we *lionize* such a great mane!

Now take Peacock's amazing surprise—
he can open a tail of jeweled eyes.
Such a stunning display
warns all rivals away
when his feathers fan out a Sir Prize.

Monarch's missing a mane and a tail.
He has nothing that shouts "You've got male!"
But perhaps you can spot
on each hind wing a dot.
It is all just a matter of scale.

WONDROUS WINGS

The magnifying glass can show
what we, as viewers, never know:
that scales are lined up in a row.

So small are monarch scales it takes
tens of thousands of dazzling flakes
to make up all these rooftop shakes.

The perfect patternings unfold
in tapestries of crimson gold.
Abstract art grown huge and bold!

Yet dyes and paints can never quite
catch that iridescent light
the wings of butterflies ignite.

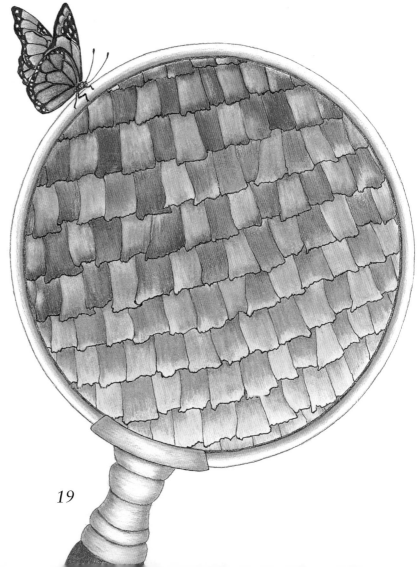

CHAOS

These are the wings
    that brushed the breeze
    that woke the wind
    that quickened the clouds
    that gathered the gale
    that swept the sea
    that stormed the shore
    and thrashed the trees
    caught in the path
    of Hurricane's wrath.

These are the wings.

THE SKYWAY TO MEXICO

Only a whisper from ancient roots,
   and cyclones of orange rise.
Good-bye to summer-sweet pursuits!
Only a whisper from ancient roots,
and billions dressed in brilliant suits
  fill skyways billed for butterflies.
Only a whisper from ancient roots,
   and cyclones of orange rise.

22

A NOTE TO THE MONARCHS

In harmony with what is beautiful and right
you come—posing on a manuscript of light.

Tiny melodies in orange, black, and white
soaring south, seeking your ancestral site.

May gentle breezes guide you in your flight.

WINTERING OVER

Amazing
Blazing
Clusters
Decorate
Entire
Forest
Groves.

Hanging
In
Jeweled
Kingdoms
Like
Magnificent
Native
Ornaments,
Patterns
Quicken
Remote
Slopes.

This
Unique,
Velvet-
Winged
X-odus
Yields
Zillions.

There are no borders
for the migrating monarch.
It is all one land.

BEFORE

The butterfly was there
before any human art was made.
Before cathedrals rose in prayer,
the butterfly was there.
Before pyramids pierced the air
or Great Wall stones were laid,
the butterfly was there.
Before any human, art was made.

SMALL MATTERS

"SIPPING SUPPER"

Though a rare treat for the monarch, watermelon juice is an excellent source of nourishment. Some monarchs will fly about 2,500 miles (4,000 kilometers) to their winter roosts, so they need a rich liquid diet—usually nectar from wild flowers—to sustain them during their flight.

"FEET TREAT"

A butterfly uses its sensitive antennae to detect the scent of plants. If it decides to land on a flower, the taste sensors in its feet tell the proboscis to uncoil and start sipping. The proboscis is a long, hollow tube kept tightly coiled under the butterfly's head.

"GATCHING A BUTTERFLY (1)"

I think of drawing as a thought with a line around it. Garden scenes were a favorite theme of mine as a child, and my memory of early drawings always seemed to include blue clouds, a radiating sun, five-petaled flowers, and various insects.

"GATCHING A BUTTERFLY (2)"

Butterflies have appeared in art since the beginning of civilization. Ancient Egyptian tombs, like the one depicted in this illustration, contained paintings and carvings of butterflies in marsh scenes on the banks of the Nile River. This limestone frieze was found in the tomb of Ka-em-Nofiet and dates from 2450 B.C. Amongst a flock of birds, the single, giant butterfly seems to hold a place of unusual significance.

"MONARCH BEGINNINGS"

Over a period of a few weeks, the female monarch will lay several hundred eggs, each no bigger than the head of a pin. She lays them on nothing but milkweed plants because her larvae are very particular eaters. With a gummy substance, she attaches the egg to the underside of a leaf, placing only one egg per leaf. The milkweed plant is the sole egg-laying place for monarchs, making it vitally important for their survival.

"WORLDLY WISE"

A lot of activity goes on inside the egg. Cells are busy multiplying! But after about five days, a caterpillar about the size of this comma (,) eats its way out. This lively comma begins chewing on the downy hairs of the milkweed, then starts grazing on the leaf. It chews and chews, getting bigger and bigger. In three weeks, it will be three thousand times greater in weight! During this feeding binge, it will stop and then burst out of its skin five times as it grows.

"GETTING READY"

The caterpillar finds a sheltered spot and anchors itself with a button of silk-like thread. Here, its fifth and final molt will produce a chrysalis. As it splits and shakes off the old caterpillar skin, the pupa hardens and turns into an exquisite jade green chrysalis with shiny gold dots. The function of these gold spots is still a mystery to scientists. *Chrysalis* comes from the Greek word *chrysos*, meaning "golden."

"FINAL FINERY"

Wondrous changes occur during the chrysalid stage. Within one to two weeks, the metamorphosis is complete. The green chrysalis darkens, becoming almost transparent. Cracks appear, then open up. The monarch splits the chrysalid case from the front near the head and emerges, clinging to the shell of its old home. Over the next two to three hours, the wings—hanging downward—expand, dry, and stiffen. A perfect adult insect (imago) is at last ready to fly.

"WHO CAN DECORATE"

The monarch begins its new life as a butterfly and flies only during the daytime. If it is raining, the monarch will seek shelter under leaves. It feeds on the sweet nectar of flowers, attracted to bright floral displays even from far away.

"OPPOSITES"

The contrast between earthbound, fat caterpillars and airborne, dainty butterflies is extreme. Caterpillars devour greenery. Butterflies are helpful pollinators, though: as they sip nectar, their bodies pick up pollen that fertilizes other flowers.

"YOU'VE GOT MALE"

Male and female monarchs are almost identical in appearance, but the hind wings of the male are marked with two small black spots, one per wing. These small patches contain scent scales and are used in courtship. Careful eyes will notice that the black veins on monarch wings are thinner in males than in females, too.

"WONDROUS WINGS"

The monarch's body and four wings are clothed in tiny scales. The order Lepidoptera (the scientific name describing all butterflies) comes from the Greek: *lepis* (scale) and *pteron* (wing). The thousands of wing scales are arranged like roof tiles, creating the colorful patterns unique to the monarch.

"CHAOS"

Edward Lorenz, an American mathematician and meteorologist, explored the idea that small changes can have dramatic effects. In 1972, at a meeting of scientists in Washington D.C., Lorenz posed the question: "Does the flap of a butterfly's wing in Brazil set off a tornado in Texas?" This idea seemed to capture the world's imagination and became known as the "butterfly effect."

"THE SKYWAY TO MEXICO"

As summer ends, the monarchs of Canada and the northern United States begin their migration. They travel great distances, some all the way from the Hudson Bay to the Gulf of Mexico. Brilliant orange clouds of monarchs snow down upon trees and fields, where the butterflies rest in the evenings. They rise again each morning, filling the skies on their way to the ancestral homeland.

"A NOTE TO THE MONARCHS"

These are the opening notes for the soprano voice in a trio sung in act 1, scene 2, from Mozart's opera *Così fan tutte*. The Italian words under these notes are "*Soave sia il vento*" ("May the wind be gentle")—my safe-travel wish for the monarchs embarking on their long and challenging journey.

"WINTERING OVER"

Branches quiver and bend under the burden of countless butterflies that have returned to Mexico to spend the winter months. They settle so closely and thickly that the trees are transformed from green to golden orange.

These monarchs will begin their northern journey in mid-March. They feed and mate along the route, and females seek out the milkweed plants on which to lay their eggs. Most of these migrating butterflies then die, and the next generation continues the journey into the northern United States and Canada.

"THERE ARE NO BORDERS"

Canada, the United States, Mexico: though monarchs have definite migration routes, they pass freely from one country to the next. To see how they migrate, scientists attach tiny, waterproof sticky tags to monarch wings. Scientists release the butterflies and chart where in North America observers find these borderless wonders.

"BEFORE"

Philosophers through the ages have discussed what is beauty and what is art. An old proverb says: "Beauty is in the eye of the beholder." What do you think? Can you see art in the butterfly's wings?